Accelerated Reader

Test # _14235_

R.L. _6.7_ Pt. _0.5_

Neanderthal

Abingdon Elementary

the
**EXTINCT
SPECIES**
collection

NEANDERTHAL

For a free color catalog describing Gareth Stevens Publishing's list of high-quality books and multimedia programs, call 1-800-542-2595 (USA) or 1-800-461-9120 (Canada). Gareth Stevens Publishing's Fax: (414) 225-0377. See our catalog, too, on the World Wide Web: http://gsinc.com

Library of Congress Cataloging-in-Publication Data

Coleman, Graham, 1963-
  [Neanderthals]
  Neanderthal / by Graham Coleman ; illustrated by
Tony Gibbons.
    p. cm. — (The extinct species collection)
  Originally published: The Neanderthals : Edgware, U.K. :
Quartz Editorial Services, 1995.
  Includes index.
  Summary: Discusses the Neanderthals, who they were, when
they lived, and how scientists have been able to find out so much
about their lifestyle.
  ISBN 0-8368-1593-9 (lib. bdg.)
  1. Neanderthals—Juvenile literature. [1. Neanderthal. 2. Man,
Prehistoric.] I. Gibbons, Tony, ill. II. Title. III. Series.
GN285.C64 1996
573.3—dc20   96-4995

First published in North America in 1996 by
Gareth Stevens Publishing
1555 North RiverCenter Drive, Suite 201
Milwaukee, Wisconsin 53212 USA

This U.S. edition © 1996 by Gareth Stevens, Inc. Created with original © 1995 by Quartz Editorial Services, 112 Station Road, Edgware HA8 7AQ U.K., under the title *The Neanderthals*.

Additional artwork by Clare Heronneau

U.S. Editors: Barbara J. Behm, Mary Dykstra

Printed in Mexico

1 2 3 4 5 6 7 8 9 99 98 97 96

the
**EXTINCT
SPECIES**
collection

NEANDERTHAL

by Graham Coleman
Illustrated by Tony Gibbons

Gareth Stevens Publishing
MILWAUKEE

Contents

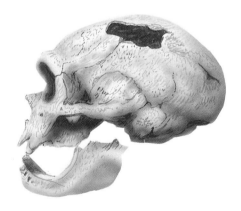

Meet Neanderthal

Homo neanderthalensis (<u>HO</u>-MO NEE-<u>AN</u>-DER THAL-<u>EN</u>-SIS), to use the full name for **Neanderthal**, lived long ago and was an early form of human life.

Neanderthal hunted large prehistoric animals, like the woolly rhinoceros and mammoth, mainly for food.

Where did **Neanderthals** live? What remains have scientists found revealing what they looked like? How intelligent were they? Why did they die out?

Do any continue to exist in remote parts of the world?

As you turn the pages of this book, you'll come face to face with both male and female **Neanderthals** and many wild creatures of their era. It's time for a fascinating journey back in time to the Ice Age.

Stocky

Nearly one hundred years ago, the French paleontologist Marcellin Boule was asked to reconstruct a **Neanderthal** from some remains. But he made many mistakes when he did this. First of all, he gave the model a spine that was not very flexible. This meant that his **Neanderthal** stood with a stoop. He also arranged the foot bones so **Neanderthal** would have walked on the outside of his feet. No wonder everyone who saw the model thought all **Neanderthals** must have been similar to apes. Only in 1957 were these errors recognized and corrected.

In fact, it has been suggested that if a **Neanderthal** could be brought back to life today, dressed in the latest clothes and given an up-to-date hairstyle and shave, he could hardly be distinguished from a modern human being. There would be just a few differences.

build

Neanderthal, as pictured in these illustrations, was about the same height as today's average adult human, but somewhat stockier in build. His forehead sloped backward at the top. **Neanderthal** also had a receding chin. He was probably much hairier than even today's hairiest men. From the study of finger bones, scientists can tell that **Neanderthal** was very skilled with his hands.

Neanderthals are thought to have been quite intelligent. However, it is not known how well they communicated with each other or whether they had conversations with one another. A bone from the base of a **Neanderthal**'s tongue was found on Mount Carmel in Israel. Scientists believe the bone reveals that **Neanderthal** probably could talk.

7

An Ice Age

Sixty thousand years ago, Earth's climate was much colder than it is today. This was the time of the great Ice Age. Although the world was not completely frozen over, **Neanderthals** had to cope with very harsh conditions. They were well adapted to cold with their stocky builds and fat reserves. Fortunately, they were also sufficiently advanced to make simple clothes from the skins of animals.

Over thousands of years, **Neanderthal** became more and more skilled at making and using tools. With tools, shelter could be built from animal skins and wood. **Neanderthal** also learned how to use fire. Scientists believe **Neanderthal** was intelligent enough to provide for the future by storing water — perhaps in the shells of hatched eggs.

people

Neanderthals took great care when burying their dead. At one burial site inside a cave in the Zagros Mountains of Iraq, a scientist found the skeletons of nine **Neanderthals**. The scientist examined the soil in which they had been buried and found different types of pollen. This showed the **Neanderthals** had been buried with several plants carefully arranged around them. The particular plants, including cornflowers, yarrow, ragwort, and thistles, were useful in the treatment of certain diseases. So perhaps **Neanderthals** thought the plants would help them after death, too.

Other **Neanderthal** remains have been found with tools and food beside them. Scientists do not know why **Neanderthals** buried their dead in this way, but it seems to show they were a caring people who had special rituals.

Neanderthal

The ability to make and use tools is something that sets humans apart from most animals. **Neanderthals** were not the first people to make tools, but they developed various new ones for the times, including sewing needles, bows and arrows, and axes.

Bone needles are among the items scientists have unearthed from **Neanderthal** sites. The needles were probably used to stitch together animal hides for simple clothing.

Weapons such as axes and harpoons were made by sharpening small stones or animal bones and attaching them to wooden sticks. Arrows could be made in this way, too, and then fired from a wooden bow.

One of the most common items made by **Neanderthal** was a scraping tool. This was probably used to prepare the wild animals that were hunted for use as food and clothing.

toolmakers

The hide had to be stripped from the carcass and the meat removed from the bones. Scraping tools might also have been used as chisels to cut the bone.

It is believed **Neanderthal** was clever enough to build rafts by tying logs together with strips of animal hide. Rafts were probably used for crossing rivers or as floating platforms from which to fish. Some experts think **Neanderthal** even mastered the technique of weaving fishing nets from strips of hide.

Neanderthals were not the first of our ancestors to discover that a spark could be created by scraping two rocks together. They did, however, develop more reliable methods of fire-making. The ability to make a good fire was important for keeping warm and for cooking. Fire could also be used as a weapon against enemies or to frighten off an attack by an animal.

Skilled

A group of **Neanderthal** hunters would keep close together until a victim was spotted. This time, it was a woolly rhinoceros, one of the largest creatures of the prehistoric world. Although a plant-eater, the woolly rhinoceros was awesome. It charged at full speed when threatened. But these **Neanderthals** were armed with a new type of weapon made by tying several medium-sized stones together. Today, this is known as a *bola*.

The hunters spread out and slowly approached the rhino. It was grazing on some scrubby grassland, unaware of the danger that it would soon have to face.

hunters

Suddenly, one of the **Neanderthals** let out a loud cry as a signal to the others that it was time to attack. The startled rhino looked up. It saw at once that it was surrounded and had no way out but to charge at the nearest hunter.

Without hesitating, the **Neanderthals** approached the massive beast and plunged their spears into its back. The rhino did not have a chance.

The woolly rhino made one last effort to rise to its feet, but it was far too weak and took its last breath.

As soon as the rhino charged, the **Neanderthals** threw their weapons at its legs, roaring with excitement as the woolly rhinoceros became entangled in the ropes. It had worked! The huge creature stumbled and fell to the ground.

The hunters then divided their prey. They used cutting tools to slice off flesh. What a feast they would have tonight! And what warm clothes the beast's woolly hide would provide for them, the women, and the children.

Neanderthal

The name *Neanderthal* comes from the Neander Valley near Düsseldorf, Germany, where **Neanderthal** remains were first discovered in 1856. A limestone quarry was being blasted when workmen noticed a few odd bones among the rubble. The bones included part of a skull that had heavy brow ridges, plus some bowed leg bones.

At the time, it would have been contrary to general religious belief in Europe even to suggest that these humanlike remains could have been much more than six thousand years old. That would have meant they predated the first human beings, Adam and Eve, according to biblical tradition.

One German scientist, therefore, suggested the bowed leg bones must have belonged to a Russian Cossack who had spent several years on horseback. How wrong this scientist was!

discovered

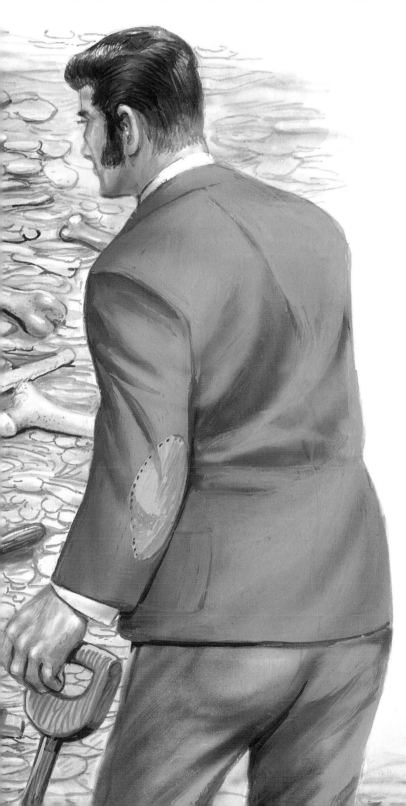

Another scientist thought the skeleton might have belonged to a man suffering from rickets. People who develop this disease have soft bones due to lack of Vitamin D. The disease causes their legs to become bowed.

Others thought the bones might have been those of someone from a modern race of wild man.

All these theories were incorrect. Thanks to later discoveries, however, new and more likely ideas have emerged.

Similar skeletal remains were dug up from pits at La Naulette and Naumur (both in Belgium). Even more bones were found in a small cave at La Chapelle aux Saints and at Le Moustier (both in France). These remains give us a fairly accurate picture of **Neanderthal**, who lived between 100,000 and 35,000 years ago.

Distant

In examining skeletal remains, scientists from time to time have made mistakes. In 1912, for instance, a jaw was found at Piltdown in Sussex, England. It seemed to be part-human, part-ape. Scientists thought they had found the missing link between humans and apes. But the remains proved to be fake.

Three main types of early humans existed on Earth prior to **Neanderthal**. All three, shown here, walked upright. They probably wore skimpy clothing or none at all. It would have been hard for them to cope with extreme temperatures. Food was not plentiful for them at the time, and they probably were malnourished. Most of them lived to only about thirty years of age.

Australopithecus (AH-STRA-LOW-PITH-EH-CUS) (**1**), like the other two types, probably lived in groups. These people communicated with grunts. They were mostly vegetarian, and tools were simple. In 1973, a female skeleton was found in Ethiopia, Africa, and named *Lucy*. She lived about three million years ago and was only 3 feet (1 meter) tall. Her brain was smaller than today's humans, too.

1

cousins

About two million years ago, **Homo erectus** (HOM-OH EE-RECT-US) (**3**), evolved. His name means "upright man." He was a hunter and toolmaker and also used fire. He was probably the first to leave Africa, since his remains have also been found in Europe and Asia.

Homo habilis (HOM-OH HAB-ILL-IS) (**2**), also from Africa, was given a name meaning "handyman" because he was skillful with tools. He was probably a hunter but may not have had the means to kill large creatures. He had a larger brain and was probably more intelligent than **Australopithecus**. **Homo habilis** is believed to have lived about two-and-a-half million years ago.

Demise of

It is not known why **Neanderthal** disappeared from the planet about thirty-five thousand years ago. But among the most likely reasons involves another group of early humans. Scientists call them **Cro-Magnons** (CROW-<u>MAG</u>-NONS).

These two types of humans lived during the same time for a few thousand years. But while **Neanderthal** lived in Africa and Europe, **Cro-Magnons** at first lived in the Middle East. They later moved to other areas.

Some scientists think **Cro-Magnon** humans may have invaded **Neanderthal** territory, and they fought with each other, as pictured.

As you can see, **Cro-Magnon** man *(right)* was taller than **Neanderthal** and may have been less hairy. In fact, in many ways, **Cro-Magnons** may have looked very similar to today's human beings.

Neanderthal

More intelligent than **Neanderthal**, **Cro-Magnon** man was able to make better weapons. It has been suggested that **Neanderthals** may have been cannibals, but that they did not eat the actual flesh of their enemies — only their brains. Perhaps they thought that by doing so, they would somehow acquire an individual's wisdom and skills. But, of course, this was not true.

Other scientists think **Cro-Magnons** may have interbred with **Neanderthals**, eventually evolving into modern humans with the scientific name of *Homo sapiens sapiens*. If that is the case, all humans alive today actually carry both **Neanderthal** and **Cro-Magnon** genes and are descended from them. You, too!

Mystery creatures

Almost all scientists agree that **Neanderthal** died out completely thirty-five thousand years ago. Yet, from time to time over the centuries, there have been reports of sightings of similar beings.

There are accounts, for instance, of the existence of hairy wild men, known as **almas**, inhabiting remote parts of Asia. As you can see through the binoculars shown in this illustration, **almas** seemed to have a snub nose, a large lower jaw, a sloping forehead, and red-brown hair. What was thought to be a dead specimen of an **alma** was discovered in 1925. His skull resembled that of **Neanderthal**. Sightings of such wild men are still reported by explorers every now and then.

So are **almas** really **Neanderthals**? Interestingly, sightings of **almas** have been close to where remains of **Neanderthals** have been dug up. But unless someone is actually able to study a live **alma**, it is not known whether **Neanderthal** still survives in some form.

Neanderthal data

There have been many finds of **Neanderthal** remains in Europe. But scientists now have evidence that **Neanderthal** also inhabited North Africa and the Middle East.

Big-browed skull

This skull of **Neanderthal** was dug up from a **Neanderthal** burial site at La Chapelle aux Saints in southwest France. Experts have put the man's age at around forty-five when he died — elderly for **Neanderthal**.

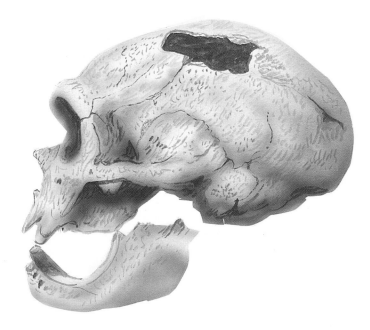

The skull was found along with a number of other bones and tools, as well as the remains of a funeral feast. The skeleton had been wedged in place with stones in a shallow grave inside a cave. Look carefully at this skull to see the very dominant brow ridges that all **Neanderthals** had.

Short but upright

A footprint found in Italy shows **Neanderthal** probably had wide, but flat, feet. Scientists also now know from reconstructions of **Neanderthal** foot bones and spines that these early people were short and walked upright. But they did not walk with a stooping apelike gait, as once thought. Scientists made this error when they studied the skeleton of an elderly **Neanderthal** who had very bad arthritis, which bent his body forward. From this one specimen, they assumed all **Neanderthals** must have walked in this manner. It was not the case.

Modern cave-dweller

One of the most important **Neanderthal** finds — nine skeletons — was in the Shanidar Cave in northern Iraq during the 1950s. The skeleton of a **Neanderthal** baby was also dug up there. At the time of the discovery, the cave was home to a modern tribesman named Miroo. Before the archaeologists arrived, Miroo, *shown here*, had no idea he was sharing his home with deceased **Neanderthals**!

Funeral flowers

While the cave at Shanidar was being excavated, archaeologists found traces of pollen that showed flowers had been carefully arranged around the dead body of a **Neanderthal**. One expert was even able to identify the pollen. It came from some plants that are familiar to us today — cornflowers, hollyhocks, and grape hyacinths, as shown *above*. Some scientists believe **Neanderthals** used herbs and other plants as a form of medicine, as well as a way to honor their dead.

Glossary

archaeologist — a scientist who studies the past by looking at remains, such as fossils, artifacts, and monuments.

Australopithecus — an early human who lived between five and two million years ago.

Cro-Magnon — an early human who lived at the same time as, and also after, Neanderthal.

Homo erectus — an early human who lived about two million years ago.

Homo habilis — an early human who lived about 2.5 million years ago.

Ice Age — a period of time between 1.5 million and 10,000 years ago, when much of Earth was covered in snow and ice.

paleontologist — a scientist who studies the past by looking at fossilized remains.

woolly rhinoceros — a huge, plant-eating creature that Neanderthal hunted for food.

Index